# Mr. Meow's Amazing ABC Adventure

**by Mr. Meow**

**Illustrated by Greg Crawford**

 Frog, Ltd.
Berkeley, California

# I'm Mr. Meow

and I'm getting ready for my **ABC** road trip. I'll need your help along the way.

I don't have a plan, but I'm going to explore America. I've packed up my Meow Mobile and I'm ready to go!

In each picture you can join me in discovering new words. I'll tell you what I see, then please join in and point out things around me I might not see.

Let's get started and we can learn together along the way.

Find the answer key to the illustrations on the last page of this book.

# Aa is for atlas.

# Bb is for blimp.

# Cc is for compass.

# Dd is for driving.

# Ee is for exercise.

# Ff
is for fishing.

# Gg is for geyser.

OLD FAITHFUL

# Hh is for hill.

**Ii** is for igloo.

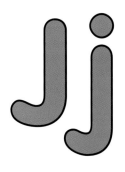

# Jj is for jump rope.

# K k is for kite.

# Ll is for lobster.

# Mm is for music.

# Nn is for newt.

Oo is for obelisk.

# P p is for picnic.

# Qq is for quartet.

# Rr is for race car.

# Ss is for snorkel.

# Tt is for tent.

# Uu is for unicycle.

# Vv

is for **v**endor.

# **Ww** is for windmill.

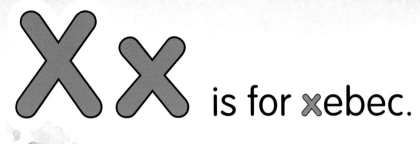

# Xx is for xebec.

XOXOCOTLÁN
2,500 MILES

# Yy is for yoga.

**Zz** is for zebra.

# Thanks so much for your help!

I wouldn't have seen so many of those sights if you hadn't come along.

Now that I'm home I need to rest and plan for our next adventure.

I hope you'll join me next time, too.

Goodbye!

## About the Author

Mr. Meow was born in the 1970s in St. Louis, Missouri. His line of cat food, Meow Mix, is known and loved by cats all over the world. Mr. Meow is renowned for bringing fun, creativity, and adventure, including his own jingle "Meow, Meow, Meow, Meow," to his Meow Mix products. This book coincides with Mr. Meow's first tour around the country in his Meow Mobile. You can look for tour dates and other fun activities at: www.meowmix.com.

## About the Illustrator

Greg Crawford has illustrated many children's books, among them *T'ai Chi for Children, What's Happening to Our Family,* and *I Can Show You I Care.* He lives in Gaysville, Vermont.

---

Published by Frog, Ltd.

Frog, Ltd. books are distributed by
North Atlantic Books, P.O. Box 12327,
Berkeley, California 94712

ISBN: 1-58394-098-7

Library of Congress Catalog Card Number 2003024284

Book design by Maxine Ressler

Printed in Singapore

1 2 3 4 5 6 7 8 9 TWP 08 07 06 05 04